for Advent and

D0662081

SACRED
SPACE

December 2, 2018 to January 13, 2019

from the website www.sacredspace.ie
Prayer from the Irish Jesuits

LOYOLA PRESS.
A JESUIT MINISTRY
Chicago

LOYOLAPRESS.
A JESUIT MINISTRY

3441 N. Ashland Avenue
Chicago, Illinois 60657
(800) 621-1008
www.loyolapress.com

Advent retreat by **Donal Neary SJ,** Editor of the Irish Sacred Heart Messenger, used with permission.

Cover art credit: Charles Harker/Moment/Getty Images.

ISBN: 978-0-8294-4700-2

18 19 20 21 22 Versa 10 9 8 7 6 5 4 3 2 1

Contents

The Presence of God

Bless all who worship you, almighty God,
from the rising of the sun to its setting:
from your goodness enrich us,
by your love inspire us,
by your Spirit guide us,
by your power protect us,
in your mercy receive us,
now and always.

How to Use This Booklet

During each week of Advent, begin by reading the "Something to think and pray about each day this week." Then go through "The Presence of God," "Freedom," and "Consciousness" steps to help you prepare yourself to hear the Word of God speaking to you. In the next step, "The Word," turn to the Scripture reading for each day of the week. Inspiration points are provided if you need them. Then return to the "Conversation" and "Conclusion" steps. Follow this process every day of Advent.

The Advent retreat at the back of this book follows a similar structure: an invitation to experience stillness, a Scripture passage and reflection points, and suggestions for prayer; you may find it useful to move back and forth between the daily reflections and the retreat.

The First Week of Advent
December 2—December 8, 2018

Something to think and pray about each day this week:

What is a hero? A hero is a person who takes action to help people. That is what the Holy Spirit calls us to do. When the Spirit descended on Mary after the angel Gabriel told her she was to be the mother of Jesus, what did she do? She took action. She packed her things and journeyed to her cousin Elizabeth. To do what? To serve her. When the Holy Spirit descended on Jesus after his baptism by John, what did he do? He took action and did what? He began his ministry and began serving. When the Spirit descended on the apostles at Pentecost, what did they do? They relinquished fear and began serving the people. Not just one group of people but all people, of all nations.

We too are called to serve, to not be afraid. With the Holy Spirit already dwelling in us, there is no time to waste. We need to take action now and assist those around us, whether it's a family member, a friend, a coworker, a stranger on the street, our environment, our nation, or our world.

—Gary Jansen, *The 15-Minute Prayer Solution*

The Presence of God

As I sit here, the beating of my heart,
the ebb and flow of my breathing,
the movements of my mind
are all signs of God's ongoing creation of me.
I pause for a moment and become aware
of this presence of God within me.

Freedom

Everything has the potential to draw from me a fuller love and life.
Yet my desires are often fixed, caught, on illusions of fulfillment.
I ask that God, through my freedom, may orchestrate my desires in a vibrant loving melody rich in harmony.

Consciousness

I ask, how am I within myself today? Am I particularly tired, stressed, or off-form? If any of these characteristics apply, can I try to let go of the concerns that disturb me?

The Word

I read the word of God slowly, a few times over, and I listen to what God is saying to me. (Please turn to the Scripture on the following pages. Inspiration points are there, should you need them. When you are ready, return here to continue.)

Conversation

I begin to talk with Jesus about the Scripture I have just read. What part of it strikes a chord in me? Perhaps the words of a friend or a story I have heard recently will slowly rise to the surface of my consciousness. If so, does the story throw light on what the Scripture passage may be trying to say to me?

Conclusion

Glory be to the Father, and to the Son, and to the Holy Spirit,
As it was in the beginning, is now and ever shall be,
World without end. Amen.

Sunday 2nd December
First Sunday of Advent
Luke 21:25–28, 34–36

"There will be signs in the sun, the moon, and the stars, and on the earth distress among nations confused by the roaring of the sea and the waves. People will faint from fear and foreboding of what is coming upon the world, for the powers of the heavens will be shaken. Then they will see 'the Son of man coming in a cloud' with power and great glory. Now when these things begin to take place, stand up and raise your heads, because your redemption is drawing near. Be on guard that your hearts are not weighed down with dissipation and drunkenness and the worries of this life, and that day does not catch you unexpectedly, like a trap. For it will come upon all who live on the face of the whole earth. Be alert at all times, praying that you may have the strength to escape all these things that will take place, and to stand before the Son of man."

- Jesus is using traditional Jewish symbolism to describe what will happen when God's final judgment occurs. He says that people will see "the Son of Man coming in a cloud." The cloud is a symbol for God's presence. Jesus' message bursts with hope and confidence because, unlike those who have reason to fear his coming, Jesus' followers will be able to hold their heads high because their liberation is at hand.

- Jesus urges me to be on guard so that my heart is not weighed down by the worries of life. What are the worries and cares of life that weigh me down today? As I prepare for a conversation with Jesus, can I bring my worries and cares to him in prayer?

Monday 3rd December
Matthew 8:5–11

When [Jesus] entered Capernaum, a centurion came to him, appealing to him and saying, "Lord, my servant is lying at home paralyzed, in terrible distress." And he said to him, "I will come and cure him." The centurion answered, "Lord, I am not worthy to have you come under my roof; but only speak the word, and my servant will be healed. For I also am a man under authority, with soldiers under me; and I say to one, 'Go,' and he goes, and to another, 'Come,' and he comes, and to my slave, 'Do this,' and the slave does it." When Jesus heard him, he was amazed and said to those who followed him, "Truly I tell you, in no one in Israel have I found such faith. I tell you, many will come from east and west and will eat with Abraham and Isaac and Jacob in the kingdom of heaven."

- "Lord, I am not worthy to have you come under my roof; but only speak the word, and my servant will be healed." These words expressed the centurion's full trust in Jesus and led to a unique commendation of this pagan man's faith. Let me spend some time pondering these words.

- People felt that they could take people who were sick—and their own sickness—to Jesus to be healed. May I do so, too, bringing my sick dear ones and all that needs healing in me to Jesus' feet.

Tuesday 4th December
Luke 10:21–24

At that same hour Jesus rejoiced in the Holy Spirit and said, "I thank you, Father, Lord of heaven and earth, because you have hidden these things from the wise and the intelligent and have revealed them to infants; yes, Father, for such was your gracious will. All things have been handed over to me by my Father; and no one knows who the Son is except the Father, or who the Father is except the Son and anyone to whom the Son chooses to reveal him." Then turning to the disciples, Jesus said to them privately, "Blessed are the eyes that see what you see! For I tell you that many prophets and kings desired to see what you see, but did not see it, and to hear what you hear, but did not hear it."

- The seventy disciples have just returned to Jesus delighted with themselves. Their mission to bring peace and reconciliation has overcome hatred and evil. But Jesus reminds the disciples that the power working in them is because of the love God has for them. Then he draws them into the circle of his divine origin: "Blessed are the eyes that see what you see!"

- Do I have a sense of my gifts having a source beyond me? Naming God as the source of all that I am may not come easily. I ask for a deeper awareness of the mystery to whom I belong.

Wednesday 5th December
Matthew 15:29–37

After Jesus had left that place, he passed along the Sea of Galilee, and he went up the mountain, where he sat down. Great crowds came to him, bringing with them the lame, the maimed, the blind, the mute, and many others. They put them at his feet, and he cured them, so that the crowd was amazed when they saw the mute speaking, the maimed whole, the lame walking, and the blind seeing. And they praised the God of Israel. Then Jesus called his disciples to him and said, "I have compassion for the crowd, because they have been with me now for three days and have nothing to eat; and I do not want to send them away hungry, for they might faint on the way." The disciples said to him, "Where are we to get enough bread in the desert to feed so great a crowd?" Jesus asked them, "How many loaves have you?" They said, "Seven, and a few small fish." Then ordering the crowd to sit down on the ground, he took the seven loaves and the fish; and after giving thanks he broke them and gave them to the disciples, and the disciples gave them to the crowds. And all of them ate and were filled; and they took up the broken pieces left over, seven baskets full.

- Lord, your compassion for all knows no bounds. No one who is brought to you fails to experience your healing touch in one manner or other.

- Small is beautiful! You use the little resources offered and fill them with abundance. All are fed. May I offer today in freedom and in love all the resources available to me, to help alleviate a love-starved world.

Thursday 6th December
Matthew 7:21, 24–27

[Jesus said to the people,] "Not everyone who says to me, 'Lord, Lord,' will enter the kingdom of heaven, but only the one who does the will of my Father in heaven. . . . "Everyone then who hears these words of mine and acts on them will be like a wise man who built his house on rock. The rain fell, the floods came, and the winds blew and beat on that house, but it did not fall, because it had been founded on rock. And everyone who hears these words of mine and does not act on them will be like a foolish man who built his house on sand. The rain fell, and the floods came, and the winds blew and beat against that house, and it fell—and great was its fall!"

- Jesus, true discipleship is as strong as the foundation on which it is built. You call me not merely to hear your word but to daily put it into action.

- Lord, when the rains fall and the floods come, threatening to overwhelm my faith in you, keep me firm, keep me rooted in you, my rock!

Friday 7th December
Matthew 9:27–31

As Jesus went on from there, two blind men followed him, crying loudly, "Have mercy on us, Son of David." When he entered the house, the blind men came to him; and Jesus said to them, "Do you believe that I am able to do this?" They said to him, "Yes, Lord." Then he touched their eyes and said, "According to your faith let it be done to you." And their eyes were opened. Then Jesus sternly ordered them, "See that no one knows of this." But they went away and spread the news about him throughout that district.

- The blind men follow you with persistence. They have one need, one prayer: "Have mercy on us."

- I too cry out to you for sight and insight. As I receive your healing touch of merciful love today, may I become an instrument of your mercy to all I encounter.

Saturday 8th December
The Immaculate Conception of the Blessed Virgin Mary
Luke 1:26–38

In the sixth month the angel Gabriel was sent by God to a town in Galilee called Nazareth, to a virgin engaged to a man whose name was Joseph, of the house of David. The virgin's name was Mary. And he came to her and said, "Greetings, favored one! The Lord is with you." But she was much perplexed by his words and pondered what sort of greeting this might be. The angel said to her, "Do not be afraid, Mary, for you have found favor with God. And now, you will conceive in your womb and bear a son, and you will name him Jesus. He will be great, and will be called the Son of the Most High, and the Lord God will give to him the throne of his ancestor David. He will reign over the house of Jacob forever, and of his kingdom there will be no end." Mary said to the angel, "How can this be, since I am a virgin?" The angel said to her, "The Holy Spirit will come upon you, and the power of the Most High will overshadow you; therefore the child to be born will be holy; he will be called Son of God. And now, your relative Elizabeth in her old age has also conceived a son; and this is the sixth month for her who was said to be barren. For nothing will be impossible with God." Then Mary said, "Here am I, the servant of the Lord; let it be with me according to your word." Then the angel departed from her.

- Years later, those surprised by the miracles of Jesus could only utter: "We have seen strange things today" (Luke 5:26). But for mother-to-be Mary, the news that the power of the Most High would cover her with its shadow was absolutely groundbreaking.

- Lord, may I grow each day in trusting your amazing annunciation to me: "You are my highly favoured one." I am not to be afraid. You rejoice in me! In the busyness of life, keep these thoughts before me. Like Mary, may I be ready to play my part in bringing you to birth.

December 9—December 15, 2018

Something to think and pray about each day this week:

Through concrete action, Jesus shows us how God loves. In the Gospels we see Jesus showing us how God loves through healing, forgiveness, mercy, and compassion. Jesus sees and responds to the deepest needs of human hearts. To a blind person he gives sight; to a paralyzed person he gives the ability to stand up and walk; to a leper and social outcast he gives cleansing and restoration to community; to a woman isolated by her illness he gives healing in both body and soul; to a person with a sinful history he gives mercy and hope for a better future.

Jesus shows us how God looks at us with eyes of compassion and love, accepting us where we are and loving us as we are. Jesus doesn't wait for people to be perfect or have their lives in order or for them to sin no more. Rather, Jesus enters the messiness of humanity and encounters people along the way in their brokenness, hurt, and mess.

—Becky Eldredge, *Busy Lives and Restless Souls*

The Presence of God

"Be still and know that I am God." Lord, your words lead us to the calmness and greatness of your presence.

Freedom

I am free. When I look at these words in writing, they seem to create in me a feeling of awe. Yes, a wonderful feeling of freedom. Thank you, God.

Consciousness

At this moment, Lord, I turn my thoughts to you.
I will leave aside my chores and preoccupations.
I will take rest and refreshment in your presence, Lord.

The Word

The word of God comes down to us through the Scriptures. May the Holy Spirit enlighten my mind and my heart to respond to the gospel teachings. (Please turn to the Scripture on the following pages. Inspiration points are there, should you need them. When you are ready, return here to continue.)

Conversation

Begin to talk with Jesus about the Scripture you have just read. What part of it strikes a chord in you? Perhaps the words of a friend—or some story you have heard recently—will slowly rise to the surface of your consciousness. If so, does the story throw light on what the Scripture passage may be trying to say to you?

Conclusion

Glory be to the Father, and to the Son, and to the Holy Spirit,
As it was in the beginning, is now and ever shall be,
World without end. Amen.

Sunday 9th December
Second Sunday of Advent

Luke 3:1–6

In the fifteenth year of the reign of Emperor Tiberius, when Pontius Pilate was governor of Judea, and Herod was ruler of Galilee, and his brother Philip ruler of the region of Ituraea and Trachonitis, and Lysanias ruler of Abilene, during the high priesthood of Annas and Caiaphas, the word of God came to John son of Zechariah in the wilderness. He went into all the region around the Jordan, proclaiming a baptism of repentance for the forgiveness of sins, as it is written in the book of the words of the prophet Isaiah, "The voice of one crying out in the wilderness:

'Prepare the way of the Lord,
    make his paths straight.
Every valley shall be filled,
    and every mountain and hill shall be made low,
and the crooked shall be made straight,
    and the rough ways made smooth;
and all flesh shall see the salvation of God.'"

- John, the cousin of Jesus, is a challenging figure. He, the messenger of God, is the sharpened arrow whose words pierce to the heart's core. Some people listened to his uncompromising message and changed the direction of their lives. But others resisted.

• Lord, this Advent, give me a welcoming heart. Help me be open to the messengers of your word, especially to those whom, at first glance, I might resist, for they are your prophets today. They urge me to change my way of thinking and living.

Monday 10th December
Luke 5:17–26

One day, while he was teaching, Pharisees and teachers of the law were sitting near by (they had come from every village of Galilee and Judea and from Jerusalem); and the power of the Lord was with him to heal. Just then some men came, carrying a paralyzed man on a bed. They were trying to bring him in and lay him before Jesus; but finding no way to bring him in because of the crowd, they went up on the roof and let him down with his bed through the tiles into the middle of the crowd in front of Jesus. When he saw their faith, he said, "Friend, your sins are forgiven you." Then the scribes and the Pharisees began to question, "Who is this who is speaking blasphemies? Who can forgive sins but God alone?" When Jesus perceived their questionings, he answered them, "Why do you raise such questions in your hearts? Which is easier, to say, 'Your sins are forgiven you,' or to say, 'Stand up and walk'? But so that you may know that the Son of Man has authority on earth to forgive sins"—he said to the one who was paralyzed—"I say to you, stand up and take your bed and go to your home." Immediately he stood up before them, took what he had been lying on, and went to his home, glorifying God. Amazement seized all of them, and they glorified God and were filled with awe, saying, "We have seen strange things today."

- The lame will leap like deer, and the tongues of the dumb will sing for joy, prophesied Isaiah. Nature itself will be renewed, with water gushing in the desert. No less will the people be joyful of heart; the whole world is poised for a makeover.

- "We have seen strange things today," said the onlookers. May Advent renew in us the wonder of the first coming of the Savior. Are we open to seeing the world strange because Jesus has come?

Tuesday 11th December
Matthew 18:12–14

"What do you think? If a man has a hundred sheep, and one of them has gone astray, does he not leave the ninety-nine on the mountains and go in search of the one that went astray? And if he finds it, truly I tell you, he rejoices over it more than over the ninety-nine that never went astray. So it is not the will of your

Father in heaven that one of these little ones should be lost."

- The savior/shepherd king lives compassion and mercy. Not one of the persons in his care is a mere statistic—the shepherd's heart is wrung and totally preoccupied if even one individual goes missing. He is the shepherd who will not rest until he has found the stray.

- But he is also a shepherd with resources of strength and power. When we feel lost or that we've gone astray, may we remember that God loves us with compassion and mercy—but also with strength and power.

Wednesday 12th December
Luke 1:39–47

In those days Mary set out and went with haste to a Judean town in the hill country, where she entered the house of Zechariah and greeted Elizabeth. When Elizabeth heard Mary's greeting, the child leapt in her womb. And Elizabeth was filled with the Holy Spirit and exclaimed with a loud cry, "Blessed are you among women, and blessed is the fruit of your womb. And why has this happened to me, that the mother of my Lord comes to me? For as soon as I heard the sound of your greeting, the child in my womb leapt for joy. And blessed is she who believed that there would be a fulfillment of what was spoken to her by the Lord." And Mary said,

"My soul magnifies the Lord,
    and my spirit rejoices in God my Savior."

- Jesus, the child that Mary is carrying, is recognized by the child in Elizabeth's womb; John leaps in recognition of the one both mothers revere as "Lord," John himself being of miraculous origin from an elderly mother.

- When two people meet who have said yes to God in their lives, like Mary and her cousin Elizabeth in today's Scripture, the new life of God that is growing in one person leaps for joy in recognition of the life of God growing in another. It is God in one greeting God in the other.

Thursday 13th December

Matthew 11:11–15

[Jesus said,] "Truly I tell you, among those born of women no one has arisen greater than John the Baptist; yet the least in the kingdom of heaven is greater than he. From the days of John the Baptist until now the kingdom of heaven has suffered violence, and the violent take it by force. For all the prophets and the law prophesied until John came;

and if you are willing to accept it, he is Elijah who is to come. Let anyone with ears listen!"

- The people were looking for Elijah; Jesus says, "John is Elijah—pay attention!" Have I been looking for an answer or a blessing that has already arrived?

- "The kingdom of heaven has suffered violence." How does the kingdom suffer today? Where do I see the kingdom of heaven, and how do I participate in it?

Friday 14th December
Matthew 11:16–19

[Jesus spoke to the crowds,] "But to what will I compare this generation? It is like children sitting in the marketplaces and calling to one another,

> 'We played the flute for you, and you did not
> dance;
> we wailed, and you did not mourn.'

For John came neither eating nor drinking, and they say, 'He has a demon'; the Son of Man came eating and drinking, and they say, 'Look, a glutton and a drunkard, a friend of tax collectors and sinners!' Yet wisdom is vindicated by her deeds."

- What was on offer from the Lord had always been happiness deep as a river, children and descendants without number. But what the people chose to do was sulk. To Jesus, their objection was the company that he ate and drank with; to John, their objection had been that he neither ate nor drank but fasted.

• Lord, I recognize something of my own response to people here. I am not always open to listening and accepting those who are different. I can so easily judge, dismiss, and reject people. I need your help today.

Saturday 15th December
Matthew 17:9a, 10–13

As they were coming down the mountain, Jesus ordered them, "Tell no one about the vision until after the Son of Man has been raised from the dead." And the disciples asked him, "Why, then, do the scribes say that Elijah must come first?" He replied, "Elijah is indeed coming and will restore all things; but I tell you that Elijah has already come, and they did not recognize him, but they did to him whatever they pleased. So also the Son of Man is about to suffer at their hands." Then the disciples understood that he was speaking to them about John the Baptist.

• Shortly before this scene, Jesus' disciples saw Jesus transfigured in glory and flanked by Moses and Elijah. They ask Jesus for confirmation regarding the role of Elijah as forerunner of the end times. Jesus' reply was unexpected in more ways than one: the real forerunner is John the Baptist, who has been treated badly. This will also be Jesus' fate.

• The coming of Jesus was meant to bring about the kingdom of God on earth with the offer of salvation for all; but the people struck out against the bearer of the message. What is my response today, when I consider God's welcome to all people?

The Third Week of Advent
December 16—December 22, 2018

Something to think and pray about each day this week:

Transition is the bridge that leads from the no longer to the not yet. Nobody can predict what that bridge is going to look like. It may be obvious and sturdy, and we may find it easily through the fogs of our bewilderment. Or it may be rickety and clearly unsafe, and we hardly dare entrust our weight to it. . . . The point is, however, that we have to cross the bridge, and as we risk that crossing, we will discover that the bridge itself is our guide and mentor, and it has everything to teach us about the path that lies ahead, beyond the transition. In fact, we will learn much more on that bridge, about ourselves, about life, and about God, in our transitions than on all the smoother pathways that we journey.

—Margaret Silf, *The Other Side of Chaos*

The Presence of God

"Come to me, all you who are weary and are carrying heavy burdens, and I will give you rest." Here I am, Lord. I come to seek your presence. I long for your healing power.

Freedom

"In these days, God taught me as a schoolteacher teaches a pupil" (Saint Ignatius).

I remind myself that there are things God has to teach me yet, and I ask for the grace to hear those things and let them change me.

Consciousness

Help me, Lord, to be more conscious of your presence. Teach me to recognize your presence in others. Fill my heart with gratitude for the times your love has been shown to me through the care of others.

The Word

God speaks to each of us individually. I listen attentively to hear what he is saying to me. Read the text a few times, then listen. (Please turn to the Scripture on the following pages. Inspiration points are there, should you need them. When you are ready, return here to continue.)

Conversation

Conversation requires talking and listening.

As I talk to Jesus, may I also learn to be still and listen.

I picture the gentleness in his eyes and the smile full of love as he gazes on me.

I can be totally honest with Jesus as I tell him of my worries and my cares.

I will open my heart to him as I tell him of my fears and my doubts.

I will ask him to help me place myself fully in his care and to abandon myself to him, knowing that he always wants what is best for me.

Conclusion

I thank God for these moments we have spent together and for any insights I have been given concerning the text.

Sunday 16th December
Third Sunday of Advent
Luke 3:10–18

And the crowds asked him, "What then should we do?" In reply he said to them, "Whoever has two coats must share with anyone who has none; and whoever has food must do likewise." Even tax collectors came to be baptized, and they asked him, "Teacher, what should we do?" He said to them, "Collect no more than the amount prescribed for you." Soldiers also asked him, "And we, what should we do?" He said to them, "Do not extort money from anyone by threats or false accusation, and be satisfied with your wages." As the people were filled with expectation, and all were questioning in their hearts concerning John, whether he might be the Messiah, John answered all of them by saying, "I baptize you with water; but one who is more powerful than I is coming; I am not worthy to untie the thong of his sandals. He will baptize you with the Holy Spirit and fire. His winnowing fork is in his hand, to clear his threshing floor and to gather the wheat into his granary; but the chaff he will burn with unquenchable fire." So, with many other exhortations, he proclaimed the good news to the people.

- John proclaimed good news to the people, but he did it "with many other exhortations." We participate with the good news by living as God's people. Might I consider this today—that I can be part of the good news for others?

- The "people were filled with expectation." They knew that something worthwhile was coming. Do I go through a typical day expecting God to act— and expecting the Holy Spirit to show me what to do?

Monday 17th December
Matthew 1:1–17

An account of the genealogy of Jesus the Messiah, the son of David, the son of Abraham. Abraham was the father of Isaac, and Isaac the father of Jacob, and Jacob the father of Judah and his brothers, and Judah the father of Perez and Zerah by Tamar, and Perez the father of Hezron, and Hezron the father of Aram, and Aram the father of Aminadab, and Aminadab the father of Nahshon, and Nahshon the father of Salmon, and Salmon the father of Boaz by Rahab, and Boaz the father of Obed by Ruth, and Obed the father of Jesse, and Jesse the father of King David. And David was the father of Solomon by the wife of Uriah, and Solomon the father of Rehoboam, and Rehoboam the father of Abijah, and Abijah the father of Asaph, and Asaph the father of Jehoshaphat, and Jehoshaphat the father of Joram, and Joram the father of Uzziah, and Uzziah the father of Jotham, and Jotham the father of Ahaz, and Ahaz the father of Hezekiah, and Hezekiah the father of Manasseh, and Manasseh the father of Amos, and Amos the father of Josiah, and Josiah the father of Jechoniah and his brothers, at the time of the deportation to Babylon. And after the deportation to Babylon: Jechoniah was the father of Salathiel, and Salathiel the father of Zerubbabel, and Zerubbabel the father of Abiud, and Abiud the father of Eliakim, and Eliakim the father of Azor, and Azor the father of Zadok, and Zadok the father of Achim, and Achim the father of Eliud, and Eliud the father of Eleazar, and Eleazar the father of Matthan, and Matthan the father of Jacob, and Jacob the father of Joseph the husband of Mary, of whom Jesus was born, who is called the Messiah. So all the generations from Abraham to David are fourteen generations, and from David to the deportation to Babylon, fourteen generations; and from the deportation to Babylon to the Messiah, fourteen generations.

- This Gospel weaves the threads of the long history that eventually brings us to Jesus. His family tree is a mix of holy and unholy figures, public sinners and outcasts. Yet each played an important role, and no one's life was insignificant to God's plan. Jesus does own his family story. He does not airbrush out any one of his ancestors. Do I?

- Lord, I thank you for all who have been a carrier of your grace to me. Let not my limitations and inadequacy impede me from believing that I am important. Let me play my part in being a carrier of your love to the world.

Tuesday 18th December
Matthew 1:18–25

Now the birth of Jesus the Messiah took place in this way. When his mother Mary had been engaged to Joseph, but before they lived together, she was found to be with child from the Holy Spirit. Her husband Joseph, being a righteous man and unwilling to expose her to public disgrace, planned to dismiss her quietly. But just when he had resolved to do this, an angel of the Lord appeared to him in a dream and said, "Joseph, son of David, do not be afraid to take Mary as your wife, for the child conceived in her is from the Holy Spirit. She will bear a son, and you are to name him Jesus, for he will save his people from their sins." All this took place to fulfill what had been spoken by the Lord through the prophet:

"Look, the virgin shall conceive and bear a son,
    and they shall name him Emmanuel,"

which means, "God is with us." When Joseph awoke from sleep, he did as the angel of the Lord commanded him; he took her as his wife, but had no marital relations with her until she had borne a son; and he named him Jesus.

- His coming is nothing less than the inauguration of a whole new (although promised) "heaven and earth" shaking epoch in the relationship between God and his people. Forgiveness of sin comes into the picture, so right away the child is accorded divine prerogative as Savior. The child's title, Emmanuel (God-with-us) designates him as the fulfillment of the promise: "I will be your God and you will be my people." His will be a leadership presence among his people.

- All these resonances come together for us as we prepare to revere the newborn child.

Wednesday 19th December
Luke 1:5–25

In the days of King Herod of Judea, there was a priest named Zechariah, who belonged to the priestly order of Abijah. His wife was a descendant of Aaron, and her name was Elizabeth. Both of them were righteous before God, living blamelessly according to all the commandments and regulations of the Lord. But they had no children, because Elizabeth was barren, and both were getting on in years. Once when he was serving as priest before God and his section was on duty, he was chosen by lot, according to the custom of the priesthood, to enter the sanctuary of the Lord and offer incense. Now at the time of the incense offering, the whole assembly of the people was praying outside. Then there appeared to him an angel of the Lord, standing at the right side of the altar of incense. When Zechariah saw him, he was terrified; and fear overwhelmed him. But the angel said to him, "Do not be afraid, Zechariah, for your prayer has been heard. Your wife Elizabeth will bear you a son, and you will name him John. You will have joy and gladness, and many will rejoice at his birth, for he will be great in the sight of the Lord. He must never drink wine or strong drink; even before his birth he will be filled with the Holy Spirit. He will turn many of the people of Israel to the Lord their God. With the spirit and power of Elijah he will go before him, to turn the hearts of parents to their children, and the disobedient to the wisdom of the righteous, to make ready a people prepared for the Lord." Zechariah said to the angel, "How will I know that this is so? For I am an old man, and my wife is getting on in years." The angel replied, "I am Gabriel. I stand in the presence of God, and I have been sent to speak to you and to bring you this good news. But now, because you did not believe my words, which will be fulfilled in their time, you will become mute, unable to speak, until the day these things occur." Meanwhile the people were waiting for Zechariah, and wondered at his delay in the sanctuary. When he did come out, he could not speak to them, and they realized that he had seen a vision in the sanctuary. He kept motioning to them and remained unable to speak. When his time of service was ended, he went to his home. After those days his wife Elizabeth conceived, and for five months she remained in seclusion. She said, "This is what the Lord has done for me when he looked favorably on me and took away the disgrace I have endured among my people."

- The promised child did finally arrive, but not without some testing of faith, given the couple's stage in life. And Zechariah learned also that the child foretold had already been designed for God's final intervention in the last days of this age: the child was being sent to prepare the way, in a role akin to that expected of the prophet Elijah. Even the name being invoked for the child—"God has shown favor"—spoke of God's intention.

- Elizabeth proclaims that the Lord has taken away her disgrace of being childless. Yet she knows that her story fits into the larger one of God's salvation. How does my life fit into this story?

Thursday 20th December

Luke 1:26–38

In the sixth month the angel Gabriel was sent by God to a town in Galilee called Nazareth, to a virgin engaged to a man whose name was Joseph, of the house of David. The virgin's name was Mary. And he came to her and said, "Greetings, favored one! The Lord is with you." But she was much perplexed by his words and pondered what sort of greeting this might be. The angel said to her, "Do not be afraid, Mary, for you have found favor with God. And now, you will conceive in your womb and bear a son, and you will name him Jesus. He will be great, and will be called the Son of the Most High, and the Lord God will give to him the throne of his ancestor David. He will reign over the house of Jacob forever, and of his kingdom there will be no end." Mary said to the angel, "How can this be, since I am a virgin?" The angel said to her, "The Holy Spirit will come upon you, and the power of the Most High will overshadow you; therefore the child to be born will be holy; he will be called Son of God. And now, your relative Elizabeth in her old age has also conceived a son; and this is the sixth month for her who was said to be barren. For nothing will be impossible with God." Then Mary said, "Here am I, the servant of the Lord; let it be with me according to your word." Then the angel departed from her.

- "Greetings, favored one! The Lord is with you." Mary, the young girl of no status, from the village of Nazareth, an utterly insignificant place, is signaled out, called, chosen, and overshadowed with God's Spirit. A unique gift, a "cause of our joy."

- "Do not be afraid": these words are for us, too. There is much to make us afraid. But nothing is impossible with God.

Friday 21st December
Luke 1:39–45

In those days Mary set out and went with haste to a Judean town in the hill country, where she entered the house of Zechariah and greeted Elizabeth. When Elizabeth heard Mary's greeting, the child leaped in her womb. And Elizabeth was filled with the Holy Spirit and exclaimed with a loud cry, "Blessed are you among women, and blessed is the fruit of your womb. And why has this happened to me, that the mother of my Lord comes to me? For as soon as I heard the sound of your greeting, the child in my womb leaped for joy. And blessed is she who believed that there would be a fulfillment of what was spoken to her by the Lord."

- Mary was a woman of faith. Elizabeth praises her, not because she has conceived the Christ but because she believed the angel's words. Let us pray to her for the strong faith we need in these troubled times. God can do what we think impossible.

- Try to imagine what it meant to Mary to find a companion in Elizabeth, an older relative who has also been blessed miraculously by God. Elizabeth understands the importance of what both of them are going through. Consider if there are any wise women in your life who can encourage your journey with God. Pray for them and thank God for them. And if there is none, ask God to send you an Elizabeth.

Saturday 22nd December

Luke 1:46–56

And Mary said,

"My soul magnifies the Lord,
    and my spirit rejoices in God my Savior,
for he has looked with favor on the lowliness of his
        servant.
    Surely, from now on all generations will call me
        blessed;
for the Mighty One has done great things for me,
    and holy is his name.
His mercy is for those who fear him

> from generation to generation.
> He has shown strength with his arm;
>> he has scattered the proud in the thoughts of
>>> their hearts.
> He has brought down the powerful from their
>> thrones,
>> and lifted up the lowly;
> he has filled the hungry with good things,
>> and sent the rich away empty.
> He has helped his servant Israel,
>> in remembrance of his mercy,
> according to the promise he made to our ancestors,
>> to Abraham and to his descendants forever."

And Mary remained with [Elizabeth] about three months and then returned to her home.

- At so many points in their history, the people of Israel were tiny in the face of menacing enemies. And at the very coming of Jesus they seemed to be at the mercy of the occupying Romans. We have the tradition of the Lord stepping in to vindicate or champion his people.

- This note will often be struck in the preaching of Jesus: the humble will be exalted and the exalted will be humbled. May we endure our trials with patience, knowing that God's justice and mercy have the last word.

The Fourth Week of Advent/Christmas
December 23—December 29, 2018

Something to think and pray about each day this week:

As all parents must, the Lady Mary and Joseph of Nazareth watched their boy begin to make up his mind about what to do with his life. There were cultural pressures, of course, one of them being the question of whether he would marry or not. His cousin John was moving toward the life led by the ancient prophets. Jesus thought seriously about his cousin's way, as his fasting and prayer in the desert suggest. But he was deeply attracted by and attached to the revealed word of God—Jesus cites the Pentateuch, the prophets, and the Psalms a lot—and he came to appreciate his vocation to serve the Father by spreading the Good News among the people. . . .

Mature discernment draws us through the mystery of the universal Savior to encounter Jesus of Nazareth, the carpenter's son. What does his human life show us? To begin with, Jesus discerned the fullness of his vocation only slowly as his life unfolded. In his public life, he gathered seventy-two disciples who were willing to go to others and tell about the Good News. From among them, he chose twelve with whom he worked on "the challenge of finding and sharing a 'mystique' of living together, of mingling and encounter, of embracing and supporting one another."

—Joseph Tetlow, SJ, *Always Discerning*

The Presence of God

"I am standing at the door, knocking," says the Lord. What a wonderful privilege that the Lord of all creation desires to come to me. I welcome his presence.

Freedom

Leave me here freely all alone / In cell where never sunlight shone / should no one ever speak to me. / This golden silence makes me free.

—Part of a poem written by a prisoner at Dachau concentration camp

Consciousness

How am I really feeling? Lighthearted? Heavyhearted? I may be very much at peace, happy to be here. Equally, I may be frustrated, worried, or angry. I acknowledge how I really am. It is the real me whom the Lord loves.

The Word

I take my time to read the word of God, slowly, a few times, allowing myself to dwell on anything that strikes me. (Please turn to the Scripture on the following pages. Inspiration points are there, should you need them. When you are ready, return here to continue.)

Conversation

Do I notice myself reacting as I pray with the word of God? Do I feel challenged, comforted, angry? Imagining Jesus sitting or standing by me, I speak out my feelings, as one trusted friend to another.

Conclusion

Glory be to the Father, and to the Son, and to the Holy Spirit,
As it was in the beginning, is now and ever shall be,
World without end. Amen.

Sunday 23rd December
Fourth Sunday of Advent
Luke 1:39–45

In those days Mary set out and went with haste to Judean town in the hill country, where she enter the house of Zechariah and greeted Elizabeth. Wh Elizabeth heard Mary's greeting, the child leaped her womb. And Elizabeth was filled with the Ho Spirit and exclaimed with a loud cry, "Blessed are y among women, and blessed is the fruit of your wom And why has this happened to me, that the moth of my Lord comes to me? For as soon as I heard t sound of your greeting, the child in my womb leape for joy. And blessed is she who believed that the would be a fulfillment of what was spoken to her the Lord."

- Two women meet, and each has received speci blessing and calling from God. Perhaps this what drew them together, what made Mary fe an urgency about visiting her cousin. This is b one example of God showing us how his holy w is accomplished not by a single person but in t context of community.

- Have I recently spoken confirmation of anoth person's gift or role in a good endeavor? Who have I called "blessed"?

Monday 24th December
Luke 1:67–79

Then his father Zechariah was filled with the Holy Spirit and spoke this prophecy:

"Blessed be the Lord God of Israel,
> for he has looked favorably on his people and
>> redeemed them.
He has raised up a mighty savior for us
> in the house of his servant David,
as he spoke through the mouth of his holy prophets
>> from of old,
> that we should be saved from our enemies and
>> from the hand of all who hate us.
Thus he has shown the mercy promised to our
>> ancestors,
> and has remembered his holy covenant,
the oath that he swore to our ancestor Abraham,
> to grant us that we, being rescued from the
>> hands of our enemies,
might serve him without fear, in holiness and
>> righteousness before him all our days.
And you, child, will be called the prophet of the
>> Most High;
> for you will go before the Lord to prepare his
>> ways,
to give knowledge of salvation to his people
> by the forgiveness of their sins.

By the tender mercy of our God,
>   the dawn from on high will break upon us,
to give light to those who sit in darkness and in the
>   shadow of death,
>   to guide our feet into the way of peace."

- Zechariah, released from his silence, bursts forth in profound praise, proclaiming the activity of God at work in our world's history. The Savior is coming! His own son will act as witness and light-bearer to the lovingkindness and mercy of the Great and Holy One.

- Lord, as I move into Christmas Eve, remind me again of how mercy is the dominant theme of how you walk with us. You are forever tender toward me. Help me grow daily in the awareness of your mercy and tenderness, which are constantly at work in my life.

Tuesday 25th December
The Nativity of the Lord (Christmas)
John 1:1–18

In the beginning was the Word, and the Word was with God, and the Word was God. He was in the beginning with God. All things came into being through him, and without him not one thing came into being. What has come into being in him was life, and the life was the light of all people. The light shines in the darkness, and the darkness did not overcome it.

There was a man sent from God, whose name was John. He came as a witness to testify to the light, so that all might believe through him. He himself was not the light, but he came to testify to the light. The true light, which enlightens everyone, was coming into the world.

He was in the world, and the world came into being through him; yet the world did not know him. He came to what was his own, and his own people did not accept him. But to all who received him, who believed in his name, he gave power to become children of God, who were born, not of blood or of the will of the flesh or of the will of man, but of God.

And the Word became flesh and lived among us, and we have seen his glory, the glory as of a father's only son, full of grace and truth. (John testified to him and cried out, "This was he of whom I said, 'He who comes after me ranks ahead of me because he was before me.'") From his fullness we have all received, grace upon grace. The law indeed was given through Moses; grace and truth came through Jesus Christ. No one has ever seen God. It is God the only Son, who is close to the Father's heart, who has made him known.

(the

- It had been said that nobody can look on the face of God and live. But now we can see his glory because, as Scripture assures us, Jesus is the perfect image of the unseen God.

- As all of us today work our way through the Gospel episodes, the realization at the back of our minds should remain: looking at the face of Christ, we are looking at the face of God.

Wednesday 26th December
Matthew 10:17–22

Beware of them, for they will hand you over to councils and flog you in their synagogues; and you will be dragged before governors and kings because of me, as a testimony to them and the Gentiles. When they hand you over, do not worry about how you are to speak or what you are to say; for what you are to say will be given to you at that time; for it is not you who speak, but the Spirit of your Father speaking through you. Brother will betray brother to death, and a father his child, and children will rise against parents and have them put to death; and you will be hated by all because of my name. But the one who endures to the end will be saved.

- Often we struggle with the opposition we face when trying to live an honest Christian life, and with the increasing duplicity that seems to surround us. Jesus knows this, yet he still sends us to take the Gospel to this difficult world. But he also promises us his assistance: he asks us not to worry!

• This makes sense only if we are doing it "because of him." We are being his disciples, following him along the path he has already trod. I ask for the grace of fortitude until the end, for myself and for those who suffer for being witnesses to Jesus. I think especially of the Christians in the Middle East.

Thursday 27th December
John 20:1–8

Early on the first day of the week, while it was still dark, Mary Magdalene came to the tomb and saw that the stone had been removed from the tomb. So she ran and went to Simon Peter and the other disciple, the one whom Jesus loved, and said to them, "They have taken the Lord out of the tomb, and we do not know where they have laid him." Then Peter and the other disciple set out and went towards the tomb. The two were running together, but the other disciple outran Peter and reached the tomb first. He bent down to look in and saw the linen wrappings lying there, but he did not go in. Then Simon Peter came, following him, and went into the tomb. He saw the linen wrappings lying there, and the cloth that had been on Jesus' head, not lying with the linen wrappings but rolled up in a place by itself. Then the other disciple, who reached the tomb first, also went in, and he saw and believed.

- As described by Benedict XVI, "The Resurrection was like an explosion of light," a "cosmic event" linking heaven and earth. But above all, it was "an explosion of love." "It ushered in a new dimension of being, . . . through which a new world emerges. . . . It is a . . . leap in the history of 'evolution' and of life in general towards a new future life, towards a new world which, starting from Christ, already continuously permeates this world of ours, transforms it and draws it to itself." The Resurrection unites us with God and others. "If we live in this way, we transform the world."

- "We proclaim the Resurrection of Christ," says Pope Francis, "when his light illuminates the dark moments of our life and we can share that with others: when we know how to smile with those who smile and weep with those who weep; when we walk beside those who are sad and in danger of losing hope; when we recount our experience of faith with those who are searching for meaning and happiness. With our attitude, with our witness, with our life, we say: Jesus is risen! Let us say it with all our soul."

Friday 28th December
Matthew 2:13–18

Now after they had left, an angel of the Lord appeared to Joseph in a dream and said, "Get up, take the child and his mother, and flee to Egypt, and remain there until I tell you; for Herod is about to search for the child, to destroy him." Then Joseph got up, took the child and his mother by night, and went to Egypt, and remained there until the death of Herod. This was to fulfill what had been spoken by the Lord through the prophet, "Out of Egypt I have called my son."

When Herod saw that he had been tricked by the wise men, he was infuriated, and he sent and killed all the children in and around Bethlehem who were two years old or under, according to the time that he had learned from the wise men. Then was fulfilled what had been spoken through the prophet Jeremiah:

"A voice was heard in Ramah,
    wailing and loud lamentation,
Rachel weeping for her children;
    she refused to be consoled, because they are no
        more."

- Starting with the scene of the holy family forced to flee into Egypt, we reflect in our prayer on the Jewish people once finding themselves in captivity in Egypt, and on their eventual release being withheld by Pharaoh until first the blood of a child flowed in every house of his own population.

- The road to the fullness of freedom (for the people, in the Promised Land) had tragic turns—as the road before him was to have for Jesus himself; as in one way or another, the road before each of us will always have.

Saturday 29th December
Luke 2:22–35

When the time came for their purification according to the law of Moses, they brought him up to Jerusalem to present him to the Lord (as it is written in the law of the Lord, "Every firstborn male shall be designated as holy to the Lord"), and they offered a sacrifice according to what is stated in the law of the Lord, "a pair of turtledoves or two young pigeons."

Now there was a man in Jerusalem whose name was Simeon; this man was righteous and devout, looking forward to the consolation of Israel, and the Holy Spirit rested on him. It had been revealed to him by the Holy Spirit that he would not see death before he had seen the Lord's Messiah. Guided by the Spirit, Simeon came into the temple; and when the parents brought in the child Jesus, to do for him what was customary under the law, Simeon took him in his arms and praised God, saying,

"Master, now you are dismissing your servant in
          peace,
     according to your word;
for my eyes have seen your salvation,
     which you have prepared in the presence of all
          peoples,
a light for revelation to the Gentiles
     and for glory to your people Israel."

And the child's father and mother were amazed at what was being said about him. Then Simeon blessed them and said to his mother Mary, "This child is destined for the falling and the rising of many in Israel, and to be a sign that will be opposed so that the inner thoughts of many will be revealed—and a sword will pierce your own soul too."

- That spirit of God who all along (according to Simeon) was master of events has finally in our own day been sent even more directly into the world by the ascended Jesus.

- Lord, may your Holy Spirit rest on me today. Like Simeon, may I too recognize that you have come in the form of a vulnerable child.

First Week of Christmas
December 30, 2018—January 5, 2019

Something to think and pray about each day this week:

Last year during our Advent Lessons, Lights, and Carols service, the priest read the genealogy of Christ. You'd think a list of forty-one names would make for a pretty dull liturgy, but for me it was the highpoint. He read it in sections. At regular intervals, between prayers and songs, there'd come a timpani roll from the choir loft, and then a few generations of names, each one pronounced gravely, as if recognizing a death. It felt like that, like a funeral for everyone. And it would have felt hopeless, but at some point the last drum roll came, and with it the sudden, shocking appearance not of yet another who would die and be gone but of Jesus who is called the Christ.

—Amy Andrews, *2017: A Book of Grace-Filled Days*

The Presence of God

"Be still, and know that I am God!" Lord, may your spirit guide me to seek your loving presence more and more for it is there I find rest and refreshment from this busy world.

Freedom

By God's grace I was born to live in freedom. Free to enjoy the pleasures he created for me. Dear Lord, grant that I may live as you intended, with complete confidence in your loving care.

Consciousness

How am I today?

Where am I with God? With others?

Do I have something to be grateful for? Then I give thanks.

Is there something I am sorry for? Then I ask forgiveness.

The Word

God speaks to each of us individually. I need to listen, to hear what he is saying to me. Read the text a few times, then listen. (Please turn to the Scripture on the following pages. Inspiration points are there, should you need them. When you are ready, return here to continue.)

Conversation

How has God's word moved me? Has it left me cold?
Has it consoled me or moved me to act in a new way?
I imagine Jesus standing or sitting beside me.
I turn and share my feelings with him.

Conclusion

I thank God for these moments we have spent together and for any insights I have been given concerning the text.

Sunday 30th December
The Holy Family of Jesus, Mary, and Joseph
Luke 2:41–52

Now every year his parents went to Jerusalem for the festival of the Passover. And when he was twelve years old, they went up as usual for the festival. When the festival was ended and they started to return, the boy Jesus stayed behind in Jerusalem, but his parents did not know it. Assuming that he was in the group of travelers, they went a day's journey. Then they started to look for him among their relatives and friends. When they did not find him, they returned to Jerusalem to search for him. After three days they found him in the temple, sitting among the teachers, listening to them and asking them questions. And all who heard him were amazed at his understanding and his answers. When his parents saw him they were astonished; and his mother said to him, "Child, why have you treated us like this? Look, your father and I have been searching for you in great anxiety." He said to them, "Why were you searching for me? Did you not know that I must be in my Father's house?" But they did not understand what he said to them. Then he went down with them and came to Nazareth, and was obedient to them. His mother treasured all these things in her heart. And Jesus increased in wisdom and in years, and in divine and human favor.

- "In my Father's house." Do I believe that the Father's house may be found within myself? If I do, I can perhaps open myself to an even greater wonder: "Those who love me will keep my word, and my Father will love them, and we will come to them and make our home with them" (John 14:23).

- Let me take in this scene slowly. Jesus is coming of age, entering his teens, and is an eager student questioning his teachers. To his mother's query—"your father and I"—he points gently to another paternity: "I must be in my Father's house." No Gospel scene shows more clearly the gradual process by which he grew into a sense of his mission. Let me savor it.

Monday 31st December
John 1:1–18

In the beginning was the Word, and the Word was with God, and the Word was God. He was in the beginning with God. All things came into being through him, and without him not one thing came into being. What has come into being in him was life, and the life was the light of all people. The light shines in the darkness, and the darkness did not overcome it. There was a man sent from God, whose name was John. He came as a witness to testify to the light, so that all might believe through him. He himself was not the light, but he came to testify to the light. The true light, which enlightens everyone, was coming into the world. He was in the world, and the world came into being through him; yet the world did not know him. He came to what was his own, and his own people did not accept him. But to all who received him, who believed in his name, he gave power to become children of God, who were born, not of blood or of the will of the flesh or of the will of man, but of God. And the Word became flesh and lived among us, and we have seen his glory, the glory as of a father's only son, full of grace and truth. (John testified to him and cried out, "This was he of whom I said, 'He who comes after me ranks ahead of me because he was before me.'") From his fullness have we all received, grace upon grace. The law indeed was given through Moses; grace and truth came through Jesus Christ. No one has ever seen God. It is God the only Son, who is close to the Father's heart, who has made him known.

- The Word of God is more than a mere communication or message coming from God; it is nothing less than God's self-communication (and at more than one level). The Word—or "Wisdom"—is a personification of God and of God the Creator ("the world came into being through him") and the source of all light and life.

- God's self-sharing extended even to his Word, Jesus, being made flesh. Jesus has joined our humanity. And our humanity is forever joined to his divinity and glory.

Tuesday 1st January
Solemnity of Mary,
the Holy Mother of God
Luke 2:16–21

So they went with haste and found Mary and Joseph, and the child lying in the manger. When they saw this, they made known what had been told them about this child; and all who heard it were amazed at what the shepherds told them. But Mary treasured all these words and pondered them in her heart. The shepherds returned, glorifying and praising God for all they had heard and seen, as it had been told them. After eight days had passed, it was time to circumcise the child; and he was called Jesus, the name given by the angel before he was conceived in the womb.

- The wonderful thing revealed in this story is that God's self-revelation as love is not to the select few but to you and me. Mary's greatness is apparent

in the fact that she took time to ponder this revelation not just in her mind but also in her heart.

• In your prayer you might ask Mary to tell you
the story of what happened and then ponder this
with her.

Wednesday 2nd January
John 1:19–28

This is the testimony given by John when the Jews
sent priests and Levites from Jerusalem to ask him,
"Who are you?" He confessed and did not deny it,
but confessed, "I am not the Messiah." And they
asked him, "What then? Are you Elijah?" He said, "I
am not." "Are you the prophet?" He answered, "No."
Then they said to him, "Who are you? Let us have an
answer for those who sent us. What do you say about
yourself?" He said,

"I am the voice of one crying out in the wilderness,
'Make straight the way of the Lord,'"
as the prophet Isaiah said.

Now they had been sent from the Pharisees. They
asked him, "Why then are you baptizing if you are
neither the Messiah, nor Elijah, nor the prophet?"
John answered them, "I baptize with water. Among
you stands one whom you do not know, the one
who is coming after me; I am not worthy to untie

the thong of his sandal." This took place in Bethany across the Jordan where John was baptizing.

- John the Baptist's mission was to emphasize the importance of Jesus over himself. This became a major characteristic of Jesus' teaching, too: humility. This means facing two realities about ourselves: that there is a very small part of us that is limited and sinful but that this must not prevent us from seeing the far greater part of ourselves that is gifted by nature and even more so by grace.

- For a few moments of prayer, be with John the Baptist and let him tell you how fortunate you are to have met Jesus. Let him tell you of his own enthusiasm about Jesus.

Thursday 3rd January
John 1:29–34

The next day he saw Jesus coming toward him and declared, "Here is the Lamb of God who takes away the sin of the world! This is he of whom I said, 'After me comes a man who ranks ahead of me because he was before me.' I myself did not know him; but I came baptizing with water for this reason, that he might be revealed to Israel." And John testified, "I saw the Spirit descending from heaven like a dove, and it remained on him. I myself did not know him, but the one who sent me to baptize with water said to me, 'He on whom you see the Spirit descend and remain is the one who baptizes with the Holy Spirit.' And I myself have seen and have testified that this is the Son of God."

- In today's Gospel reading, John the Baptist speaks of God as the one who sent him and the Spirit as the one who descends on Jesus and remains with him. As Karl Rahner expressed it, "What is central to all Theology and Spirituality is that the three persons of the Trinity want to reveal themselves to you."

- For some moments of prayer be with Mary and John as they experience the purpose of the Old Testament unfolding before their eyes. This is the plan of the three persons of the Trinity to reveal themselves to you.

Friday 4th January
John 1:35–42

The next day John again was standing with two of his disciples, and as he watched Jesus walk by, he exclaimed, "Look, here is the Lamb of God!" The two disciples heard him say this, and they followed Jesus. When Jesus turned and saw them following, he said to them, "What are you looking for?" They said to him, "Rabbi" (which translated means Teacher), "where are you staying?" He said to them, "Come and see." They came and saw where he was staying, and they remained with him that day. It was about four o'clock in the afternoon. One of the two who heard John speak and followed him was Andrew, Simon Peter's brother. He first found his brother Simon and said to him, "We have found the Messiah" (which is translated Anointed). He brought Simon to Jesus, who looked at him and said, "You are Simon son of John. You are to be called Cephas" (which is translated Peter).

- Matthew, Mark, and Luke see the Christian vocation to be expressed in the words, "repent, and believe in the good news" (Mark 1:14–15). John, however, sees our vocation to be an answer to Jesus' words, "Come and see." This is an invitation to come to know Jesus as God's love made visible that the Holy Spirit wants to lead you into (John 16:13–15).

- If you have time to pray with today's Gospel, you might quiet yourself for a short while by listening to the sounds around you. Then let Jesus say the words, "Come and see" to you several times, pausing so that you hear the tone of his voice and see the expression on his face.

Saturday 5th January

John 1:43–51

The next day Jesus decided to go to Galilee. He found Philip and said to him, "Follow me." Now Philip was from Bethsaida, the city of Andrew and Peter. Philip found Nathanael and said to him, "We have found him about whom Moses in the law and also the prophets wrote, Jesus son of Joseph from Nazareth." Nathanael said to him, "Can anything good come out of Nazareth?" Philip said to him, "Come and see." When Jesus saw Nathanael coming toward him, he said of him, "Here is truly an Israelite in whom there is no deceit!" Nathanael asked him, "Where did you get to know me?" Jesus answered, "I saw you under the fig tree before Philip called you." Nathanael replied, "Rabbi, you are the Son of God! You are the King of Israel!" Jesus answered, "Do you believe because I told you that I saw you under the fig tree? You will see greater things than these." And he said to him, "Very truly, I tell you, you will see heaven opened and the angels of God ascending and descending upon the Son of Man."

• Today's reading is all about the call of the Christian, about your call to be with Jesus as your friend. Reflect on what it means to be a Christian today by pondering on how the Gospels are all about Jesus as he went about making friends to lead us into his own relationship with his Father.

- In the light of this, be with Jesus in a quiet place and ask him about the dream he has for you as his friend.

The Epiphany of Our Lord /
The Second Week of Christmas
January 6, 2019—January 13, 2019

Something to think and pray about each day this week:

Would you have noticed the star in the sky? Or would you have been too busy and distracted? Would you have been quiet and still enough to look up, to contemplate the stars and the greatness of the universe? To stop and be in awe? To breathe in the cold night air? To notice that something was happening? Sometimes we wait for God to come, but what we really need to do is be quiet and attentive enough to notice and discern what he is already doing. And, more often than not, God is found where we least expect him.

—Karen Beattie, *2018: A Book of Grace-Filled Days*

The Presence of God
Dear Jesus, today I call on you, but not to ask for anything. I'd like only to dwell in your presence. May my heart respond to your love.

Freedom
God my creator, you gave me life and the gift of freedom. Through your love I exist in this world. May I never take the gift of life for granted. May I always respect others' right to life.

Consciousness
I ask how I am today. Am I particularly tired, stressed, or anxious? If any of these characteristics apply, can I try to let go of the concerns that disturb me?

The Word
The word of God comes down to us through the Scriptures. May the Holy Spirit enlighten my mind and my heart to respond to the gospel teachings. (Please turn to the Scripture on the following pages. Inspiration points are there, should you need them. When you are ready, return here to continue.)

Conversation

I begin to talk with Jesus about the Scripture I have just read. What part of it strikes a chord in me? Perhaps the words of a friend—or some story I have heard recently—will rise to the surface in my consciousness. If so, does the story throw light on what the Scripture passage may be saying to me?

Conclusion

Glory be to the Father, and to the Son, and to the Holy Spirit,
As it was in the beginning, is now and ever shall be,
World without end. Amen.

Sunday 6th January
The Epiphany of the Lord
Matthew 2:1–12

In the time of King Herod, after Jesus was born in Bethlehem of Judea, wise men from the East came to Jerusalem, asking, "Where is the child who has been born king of the Jews? For we observed his star at its rising, and have come to pay him homage." When King Herod heard this, he was frightened, and all Jerusalem with him; and calling together all the chief priests and scribes of the people, he inquired of them where the Messiah was to be born. They told him, "In Bethlehem of Judea; for so it has been written by the prophet:

'And you, Bethlehem, in the land of Judah,
    are by no means least among the rulers of
        Judah;
for from you shall come a ruler
    who is to shepherd my people Israel.'"

Then Herod secretly called for the wise men and learned from them the exact time when the star had appeared. Then he sent them to Bethlehem, saying, "Go and search diligently for the child; and when you have found him, bring me word so that I may also go and pay him homage." When they had heard the king, they set out; and there, ahead of them, went the star that they had seen at its rising, until it stopped over the place where the child was. When they saw that the star had stopped, they were overwhelmed with joy. On entering the house, they saw the child with Mary his mother; and they knelt down and paid him homage. Then, opening their treasure chests, they offered him gifts of gold, frankincense, and myrrh. And having been warned in a dream not to return to Herod, they left for their own country by another road.

- The story told in today's Gospel is about people being called to follow their star to find the fullness of life only Jesus can give. "I came that they may have life, and have it abundantly" (John 10:10).

- You may not have thought much about the nature of the star you follow. With a view to clarifying this, it may be worthwhile to ask yourself what you want for your children, your family, or your friends. Having done this, you might talk to Jesus about whether this is what he wants for you—if this is the star he wishes you to follow.

Monday 7th January
Matthew 4:12–17, 23–25

Now when Jesus heard that John had been arrested, he withdrew to Galilee. He left Nazareth and made his home in Capernaum by the sea, in the territory of

Zebulun and Naphtali, so that what had been spoken through the prophet Isaiah might be fulfilled:

"Land of Zebulun, the land of Naphtali,
    on the road by the sea, across the Jordan,
        Galilee of the Gentiles—
the people who sat in darkness
    have seen a great light,
and for those who sat in the region and shadow of
        death
    light has dawned."

From that time Jesus began to proclaim, "Repent, for the kingdom of heaven has come near."

- Now that John is in prison, Jesus begins to preach the same message John preached: "Repent, for the kingdom of heaven has come near." There is continuity among God's prophets and preachers; even his Son takes up the baton John has had to set down.

- Holy Spirit, show me how my own calling and ministry fit into the long story of your work in this world.

Tuesday 8th January
Mark 6:34–44

As he went ashore, he saw a great crowd; and he had compassion for them, because they were like sheep without a shepherd; and he began to teach them many things. When it grew late, his disciples came to him and said, "This is a deserted place, and the hour is now very late; send them away so that they may go into the surrounding country and villages and buy something for themselves to eat." But he answered them, "You give them something to eat." They said to him, "Are we to go and buy two hundred denarii worth of bread, and give it to them to eat?" And he said to them, "How many loaves have you? Go and see." When they had found out, they said, "Five, and two fish." Then he ordered them all to get all the people to sit down in groups on the green grass. So they sat down in groups of hundreds and of fifties. Taking the five loaves and the two fish, he looked up to heaven, and blessed and broke the loaves, and gave them to his disciples to set before the people; and he divided the two fish among them all. And all ate and were filled; and they took up twelve baskets full of broken pieces and of the fish. Those who had eaten the loaves numbered five thousand men.

- Notice that Jesus allows the disciples to grow uncomfortable; he gives them time to assess the need of the crowd and bring it to him. A proper leader has a better plan, doesn't he—thinks through all the logistics ahead of time? Had you been a disciple in that situation, how would you have responded?

- Jesus began with the food that was already there. Help me, Lord, to be aware of what you have provided and, with gratitude, may I continue forward with faith.

Wednesday 9th January
Mark 6:45–52

Immediately he made his disciples get into the boat and go on ahead to the other side, to Bethsaida, while he dismissed the crowd. After saying farewell to them, he went up on the mountain to pray. When evening came, the boat was out on the sea, and he was alone on the land. When he saw that they were straining at the oars against an adverse wind, he came towards them early in the morning, walking on the sea. He intended to pass them by. But when they saw him walking on the sea, they thought it was a ghost and cried out; for they all saw him and were terrified. But immediately he spoke to them and said, "Take heart, it is I; do not be afraid." Then he got into the boat with them and the wind ceased. And they were utterly astounded, for they did not understand about the loaves, but their hearts were hardened.

- Imagine yourself in the boat with the disciples and listen to what they say as the storm develops. Listen to them as they observe the figure coming across the water!

- Jesus saw that they were straining at the oars—
  that they were in difficulty. Yet he intended to pass
  by them. He shows care for their well-being yet
  it seems that he waits for their response. Ponder
  what these scene may indicate about how God
  watches over us.

Thursday 10th January
Luke 4:14–22a

Then Jesus, filled with the power of the Spirit, returned to Galilee, and a report about him spread
through all the surrounding country. He began to
teach in their synagogues and was praised by everyone. When he came to Nazareth, where he had been
brought up, he went to the synagogue on the sabbath day, as was his custom. He stood up to read, and
the scroll of the prophet Isaiah was given to him. He
unrolled the scroll and found the place where it was
written:

"The Spirit of the Lord is upon me,
    because he has anointed me
        to bring good news to the poor.
He has sent me to proclaim release to the captives
    and recovery of sight to the blind,
        to let the oppressed go free,
to proclaim the year of the Lord's favor."

And he rolled up the scroll, gave it back to the atten-
dant, and sat down. The eyes of all in the synagogue
were fixed on him. Then he began to say to them,
"Today this scripture has been fulfilled in your hearing." All spoke well of him and were amazed at the
gracious words that came from his mouth.

- Of all the texts available to him, Jesus chose this
  ringing description of his mission from Isaiah: to
  bring good news to the poor, to give sight to the
  blind, to let the oppressed go free. As I reflect on
  Jesus' own understanding of his mission, I look at
  our world as we struggle with so many social is-
  sues: the welcome of refugees and migrants to our
  countries and communities, the growing inequal-
  ity between those who have and those who have
  not, the destruction of the environment. What is
  the Spirit of the Lord sending me to do, as a fol-
  lower of Jesus? I ask for the grace not to be deaf to
  his call, but to carry it out with great generosity.

- Jesus went to synagogue on the sabbath day,
  "which was his custom." We tend to forget that
  Jesus was a practicing Jew of his time. He began
  his ministry in the midst of the people of his community and faith. What are the advantages and
  disadvantages of this? Can I relate to Jesus' situation in this scene?

Friday 11th January

Luke 5:12–16

Once, when he was in one of the cities, there was a man covered with leprosy. When he saw Jesus, he bowed with his face to the ground and begged him, "Lord, if you choose, you can make me clean." Then Jesus stretched out his hand, touched him, and said, "I do choose. Be made clean." Immediately the leprosy left him. And he ordered him to tell no one. "Go," he said, "and show yourself to the priest, and, as Moses commanded, make an offering for your cleansing, for a testimony to them." But now more than ever the word about Jesus spread abroad; many crowds would gather to hear him and to be cured of their diseases. But he would withdraw to deserted places and pray.

- Jesus sent the leper to the priest because a priest had to verify that a person was clean and healed before admitting the person back into the community. Healing always involves more than physical health. Consider the areas of life affected by a prolonged illness.

- After such a miracle, Jesus might have remained to receive the awe and praise of the people and to keep working among them. But he recognized that his source was time with the Father. If Jesus needed prayer, can I neglect it for myself?

Saturday 12th January

John 3:22–30

After this Jesus and his disciples went into the Judean countryside, and he spent some time there with them and baptized. John also was baptizing at Aenon near Salim because water was abundant there; and people kept coming and were being baptized—John, of course, had not yet been thrown into prison. Now a discussion about purification arose between John's disciples and a Jew. They came to John and said to him, "Rabbi, the one who was with you across the Jordan, to whom you testified, here he is baptizing, and all are going to him." John answered, "No one can receive anything except what has been given from heaven. You yourselves are my witnesses that I said, 'I am not the Messiah, but I have been sent ahead of him.' He who has the bride is the bridegroom. The friend of the bridegroom, who stands and hears him, rejoices greatly at the bridegroom's voice. For this reason my joy has been fulfilled. He must increase, but I must decrease."

• In this situation we see the typical need people have of knowing who is "in" and who is "out." Their loyalty to John was commendable but misplaced. What gets in the way of our being open to God's graces coming through many people and in various ways?

- John knew that his role in the sacred drama would soon fade, and he accepted that. What would diminishment look like in my life? How will I know when it is my time to decrease, and how can I prepare my heart to respond graciously?

Sunday 13th January
The Baptism of the Lord
Luke 3:15–16, 21–22

As the people were filled with expectation, and all were questioning in their hearts concerning John, whether he might be the Messiah, John answered all of them by saying, "I baptize you with water; but one who is more powerful than I is coming; I am not worthy to untie the thong of his sandals. He will baptize you with the Holy Spirit and fire." Now when all the people were baptized, and when Jesus also had been baptized and was praying, the heaven was opened, and the Holy Spirit descended upon him in bodily form like a dove. And a voice came from heaven, "You are my Son, the Beloved; with you I am well pleased."

- Jesus came to baptize us with the Holy Spirit and with fire. Such an encounter is rarely calm and filled with certainty. It's interesting that Jesus, who was following God's will, received the confirmation of the Father saying, "You are my Son, the

Beloved . . ." Baptism brings change and activity, and it calls for courage and faith.

- Can you pause today and allow God's words to linger with you: "You are my beloved child . . ."?

An Advent Retreat

Welcome to our Advent retreat, "Messengers of Joy." The word *Advent* is taken from the Latin word *adventus*, which means "coming." Advent gives us an opportunity to wait in joyful expectation for the coming of Jesus, who is Emmanuel, God with us. The coming of God into the world as a child reminds us a real treasure of our faith: joy. The season of Advent offers an opportunity to take a step back from the busyness of life, to slow down, to wait and ponder, so that we can enter joyfully the mystery of Christmas, a time of celebration and rejoicing for all Christians.

To guide our prayer this Advent, we will reflect on some familiar moments in the Christmas story, using Scripture narrative from the book of Isaiah and the Gospel of Luke. During this time of waiting, we are invited to spend time in prayer and reflection, contemplating more deeply the mystery of Christmas so that we are truly ready for the arrival of Jesus. We wait expectantly with all God's people for the coming of Christ. We wait especially with those who played a role in his coming—Isaiah, Zechariah, Elizabeth, Mary, and the shepherds—noticing how the joyful message of Jesus' coming was first revealed.

Isaiah's prophecy about the birth of Jesus was a foretelling of great joy. It revealed God's plan from

Old Testament times to send a Messiah into the world. The angel of the Lord who appeared to Zechariah also came with a message of joy, announcing that many would rejoice at the birth of John the Baptist, the one who would prepare the way for the Lord.

Indeed, John the Baptist himself, even as a child in the womb, expressed great joy when Mary visited his mother Elizabeth. And once again, when Mary herself gave birth to the Savior, it was as "good news of great joy" that the angels announced it to the shepherds.

It is through hearing these stories afresh that we may be able to experience what it is to be a messenger of joy in this season of preparation. As we begin this retreat, you might like to examine your own thoughts and feelings surrounding this theme of joy. Do you feel joyful about the coming celebrations of the birth of Christ? Or are busyness and seasonal stress overshadowing your life at the moment? This Advent, we invite you to discover anew the joy of Christ that was spread through these remarkable men and women that first Christmas.

As we begin this Advent journey, we should ask ourselves how the following weeks will bring us closer to Jesus:

- What do you hope to gain from this retreat?
- How do you see Jesus?

- How would you express Jesus if someone asked you to?
- How would you address him?

Practicalities

We start with some practical hints that might help you if you haven't made a retreat like this before, or that might act as reminders if you have. These tips fall under three headings: how, when, and what.

One "how" question to consider is how much time are you able to devote to each session of the retreat? It's good to decide this in advance and try to stick to your decision. Don't give up too soon if the prayer seems a little dull or continue too long if it seems to be going well. The material presented in each of these session lasts 20 to 25 minutes, but you might want to take a little extra time beforehand to prepare yourself, or some time afterward to stay in prayer. The important thing is to choose a time that you can comfortably fit into your routine.

A good "when" question to ask is what time of day is best for you to pray. Would you seek out time in the morning, evening, or the middle of the day? This might also lead to another question: Where will you find it easiest to pray and reflect?

Finally, under the heading of "what," ask yourself what you hope to gain from this retreat. What are the gifts and graces you hope to receive from God during these times of prayer? Make sure you start the prayer by asking God for these or for whatever else God wants to give you.

Before you begin each time of prayer, become aware of God welcoming you to meet him in this way. Become aware, also, of all those others around the world who are praying this retreat alongside you.

Session 1: Waiting in Joy

Invitation to Stillness

As you begin this time of reflection, pause for a few moments and let your attention focus on your breathing. Notice the rhythm as you slowly breathe in and breathe out. As you breathe in, let the word *love* echo on the in-breath, conscious that God breathes love into your being. On the out-breath, echo the word *thanks*. Hold the breath for a few short moments and allow these words, *love* and *thanks*, to fill you and to echo in your mind and heart.

Reading

Isaiah 52:7–10

How beautiful upon the mountains
    are the feet of the messenger who announces
        peace,
who brings good news,

who announces salvation,
who says to Zion, "Your God reigns."
Listen! Your sentinels lift up their voices,
together they sing for joy;
for in plain sight they see
the return of the LORD to Zion.
Break forth together into singing,
you ruins of Jerusalem;
for the LORD has comforted his people,
he has redeemed Jerusalem.
The LORD has bared his holy arm
before the eyes of all the nations;
and all the ends of the earth shall see
the salvation of our God.

Reflect

- Looking forward is a lovely thing, as when we are expecting a birth in the family, beginning a new job, or preparing for marriage. We daydream about it, and we talk about it. The prophets daydreamed and talked about the coming of the Messiah. Looking forward gave them great enjoyment. And it's the same for us. We look forward to sharing in the Christmas spirit with our family and in joining the Christmas prayer in the church.

- The people of Israel knew what they were looking forward to: peace, comfort, and salvation. What about us today? We too want peace. And we know many people who need the comfort of friends, the gift of health, the warmth of faith. We need to be saved from evil in the world, and Jesus' birth promises that salvation.

- Do we know that we will receive these gifts? Yes and no. It is true that Jesus never ceases to surprise us with love, healing, and forgiveness. But people can still be left in pain at Christmas. We can bring gifts as well as receive them. Will we do something good for others at this time of year? Will we surprise others through our gentle words, good deeds, and kind actions this Christmas? We can bring the joy of Jesus and the joy of the season into the lives of many. We can help forward God's reign of love and justice—and know that our God reigns.

Talk to God

- Perhaps something has struck you during this reflection time. This is an excellent starting point. Stay with it and make it personal. But don't forget, first of all, to put yourself in the presence of God. Take your time: there is no hurry.

- Isn't there something lovely about anticipating Christmas? Expectant parents so delighted that their child will soon be born are telling everyone about it. And how much pleasure their good news brings. Can you allow your heart to lift at the fore-telling of the joy of Jesus' coming?

- The people wait for the Lord as a watchman waits for daybreak. We can't hurry the dawn, but we know it will come. Sometimes all we can do is wait. It might be waiting for something good to happen, or we might just be waiting for life to get better. Whatever the case, we can bring our patient waiting to God.

O Wisdom,
Lord and Ruler,
Root of Jesse,
Key of David,
Rising Sun,
King of the Nations,
Emmanuel, Come Jesus.

Session 2: Waiting in Silence
Invitation to Stillness
For a few moments of stillness, settle yourself in a comfortable position. Allow yourself to become quiet within. Listen attentively to the different sounds you hear and to your inner voice. Maybe you can hear your own heartbeat. As you relax into listening, try to become aware that God is near, within you, making his home in your heart.

Reading
Luke 1:11–16

Then there appeared to him an angel of the Lord, standing at the right side of the altar of incense. When Zechariah saw him, he was terrified; and fear overwhelmed him. But the angel said to him, "Do not be afraid, Zechariah, for your prayer has been heard. Your wife Elizabeth will bear you a son, and you will name him John. You will have joy and gladness, and many will rejoice at his birth, for he will be great in the sight of the Lord. He must never drink wine or strong drink; even before his birth he will be filled with the Holy Spirit. He will turn many of the people of Israel to the Lord their God."

Reflect

- Whatever this angel was like, he terrified Zechariah at first. Zechariah was a man both honored and shamed. He had not yet fathered a child, and both he and his wife would have been mocked for that. But it was an honor to be chosen to go into the Holy of holies, an inner room in the temple where the tabernacle was located. In today's terms it would be like being chosen to be principal celebrant at a big liturgy, or the head sacristan! When Zechariah saw the angel, terror took hold of him. But he was still able to hear the angel's words about joy. He heard and listened.

• Zechariah later doubted that he and Elizabeth could possibly have a child. Unlike Mary—who wondered but did not doubt—he was chastised for doubting and was struck dumb. He was reduced to silence, and in that silence he heard the truth and kept it in his heart until he would name his child. We often need silence before we can hear the truth. Indeed, *listen* and *silent* contain the exact same letters!

• Zechariah's prayer had been heard. He knew he would have a child, John the Baptist, who would announce the Savior and prepare his way by turning people to God. Though, for the moment, Zechariah had to keep his holy secret in the silence of his heart, the joy of telling the world would come later. Our Advent silence, when we choose to take time away from the busyness of the festive preparations to listen to God, will increase the joy in our hearts this Christmas.

Talk to God

• The Lord calls me by the name my parents gave me at birth. They gave me a name to last through my earthly life and into eternity. The Lord sanctifies it, as we hear in the words of the Book of

Revelation: "I will write on you the name of my God . . . and my own new name" (Revelation 3:12). God knows me by this name. It is mine. Everyone's name is sacred. How does your name throw light on your identity? Is it the name of an ancestor, of a saint, of someone popular at the time you were born?

- In a few moments of silence now, I can listen to God, who longs to speak to my heart. God can be found in ordinary life, where we live, in the sounds of people and nature. I can feel his presence in my heart when I quiet my mind and silence my voice. Jesus himself often went to a quiet place to pray in silence. There he found renewed strength to share with everyone he met the fullness of his life with the Father.

- Zechariah and Elizabeth prayed for a long time for a child. Maybe they had given up. Can I remain faithful in prayer, knowing that there is always an answer and that the answer may take time coming or come in a way I don't expect? As someone once marveled, "I got nothing I asked for and everything I needed."

O Wisdom,
Lord and Ruler,
Root of Jesse,
Key of David,

Rising Sun,
King of the Nations,
Emmanuel, Come Jesus.

Session 3: Waiting in Community
Invitation to Stillness

For a few moments settle yourself and let your body and mind become still. Allow all your attention to focus on how you are feeling, noticing how you feel in the different parts of your body. As you do so, give it all to God, who is present to you now just as you are, and beholds you in tremendous love.

Reading
Luke 1:39–46

In those days Mary set out and went with haste to a Judean town in the hill country, where she entered the house of Zechariah and greeted Elizabeth. When Elizabeth heard Mary's greeting, the child leapt in her womb. And Elizabeth was filled with the Holy Spirit and exclaimed with a loud cry, "Blessed are you among women, and blessed is the fruit of your womb. And why has this happened to me, that the mother of my Lord comes to me? For as soon as I heard the sound of your greeting, the child in my womb leapt for joy. And blessed is she who believed that there would be a fulfillment of what was spoken to her by the Lord."

Reflect

- Mary went to visit her cousin Elizabeth, who appreciated the company and help of someone in a similar situation. Their time together was joyful. Can you think of a time somebody came to help you or you went to help another? Hospitality, whether we give it or receive it, lifts the spirit and cultivates gratitude. Spending quality time visiting a friend can be a joyful experience, as can spending quality time with God.

- Elizabeth's joy came not just from Mary's presence but from experiencing the presence of the Holy Spirit. When we share our presence with other people, we also share the gifts of the Spirit, big and small, which we enjoy. It is important to acknowledge and say yes to the gifts God has given us and to cultivate them so that they can yield fruit for the kingdom of God. As we hear in Galatians: "The fruit of the Spirit is love, joy, peace, patience, kindness, generosity, faithfulness, gentleness, and self-control" (5:22–23).

- The baby leapt in Elizabeth's womb, and that image is richly symbolic. It indicates the meeting of the Old and New Testaments. John, the last of the prophets in the Old Testament tradition, meets the Messiah, the new prophet, and leaps with joy in the womb. This joy, Good News for all people, has spread through the centuries to this very day.

Talk to God

- Both Elizabeth and Mary knew that God was intervening in their lives in a profound way. They likely spent time pondering the mystery of it. No doubt they talked for hours, wondering about the sons who would soon be the focus of their lives. Put yourself in the scene and try to imagine what both women are saying. Can you think of how God may be intervening in your life at the present time?

- The first words of Elizabeth to Mary were to bless her and to give thanks to God. She acknowledged Mary's faith, how she heard the word of God and believed it. Their shared prayer encouraged both of them to believe that all that was promised would be fulfilled. Our prayer can be a blessing that we send to everyone we think of today. Do you want to ask God for a particular intention or blessing?

- We never hear of Elizabeth and Mary meeting again. Their sons would meet, and Jesus would say of John that nobody better was ever born. Jesus would have heard from Mary about her visit to Elizabeth. He would have known there was something special about John, just as there is something special about each of us. Take a few moments to get in touch with your unique talents and abilities, to ponder how you can use them to bring Good News to those you encounter this Christmas.

O Wisdom,
Lord and Ruler,
Root of Jesse,
Key of David,
Rising Sun,
King of the Nations,
Emmanuel, Come Jesus.

Session 4: Waiting for God's Word
Invitation to Stillness
Take a few moments to be still and to settle yourself into a comfortable position. Close your eyes and imagine all your worries, distractions, and concerns fading away. As you notice the silence in yourself, let yourself become conscious of God intimately present within you at this moment, present in your heart and in the place where you now pray.

Reading
Luke 2:8–20

In that region there were shepherds living in the fields, keeping watch over their flock by night. Then an angel of the Lord stood before them, and the glory of the Lord shone around them, and they were terrified. But the angel said to them, "Do not be afraid; for see—I am bringing you good news of great joy for all the people: to you is born this day in the city of David a Savior, who is the Messiah, the Lord. This will be a sign for you: you will find a child wrapped in bands of cloth and lying in a manger." And suddenly there was with the angel a multitude of the heavenly host, praising God and saying,

"Glory to God in the highest heaven,
    and on earth peace among those whom he
        favors!"

When the angels had left them and gone into heaven, the shepherds said to one another, "Let us go now to Bethlehem and see this thing that has taken place, which the Lord has made known to us." So they went with haste and found Mary and Joseph, and the child lying in the manger. When they saw this, they made known what had been told them about this child; and all who heard it were amazed at what the shepherds told them. But Mary treasured all these words and pondered them in her heart. The shepherds returned, glorifying and praising God for all they had heard and seen, as it had been told them.

Reflect

- The angels, God's heavenly messengers, told the shepherds something remarkable, that they would find a baby boy lying in a manger who is both Messiah and Lord, God and Savior! The shepherds opened themselves to this mystery of love, the news of the coming of the One who saves. Even the sheep heard the news! The whole earth moved in joy this Bethlehem night. Still, it took the world a long time to realize that Jesus' birth was good news for all humanity. The gospel is joy to the world—a message of love, calling us to peace and justice and to the celebration of the divine in our lives. The joy of the gospel is the deepest joy. It embraces all other joys so that the divine and the human are one.

- The shepherds went in faith, not to gawk out of mere curiosity but to hear more intensely what the Lord had made known to them through the angels. There is a message for us, too, each year from the Lord. Christmas is first and foremost Christ's visit to us. His intimate presence is our first Christmas present. Sometimes, though, we can get so busy that we fail to see this. Perhaps this Christmas we can each make a journey to a Bethlehem of our own: a place of special meaning, faith-filled time spent with a friend, a family rosary at home, a restful meditation. It is in Bethlehems such as these that we can learn the Lord's message to us this year.

- In the Gospel, Mary rarely speaks. She does, however, ponder a lot. Being the mother of Jesus gives her much cause for reflection and wonder. She ponders both in times of joy and in times of sorrow, and always in the presence of God. His wisdom is her wisdom. Let it be ours too this Christmas. We often wonder and marvel at the love of another person for us. Let's be astonished at the amazing love for us that God shows through the birth and life of Jesus.

Talk to God

- Look long at the sky and you will see and hear the voices of angels! Creation is the first word of God. Its color and beauty remind us of God's beauty; its storms and hurricanes remind us that we are not in charge and that this is God's world. All is charged with the glory of God.

- The next word of God, so full of life and meaning, was the Word made flesh, child of God just like us. This powerful Word communicated through the silence of a little child. For us God became human, a newborn baby lying in a manger. So much can be heard in silence, so much echoes in the "sound" of silence. Take some time to contemplate the magnitude of this mystery.

• The poor shepherds had no social status. People had little time for them. We don't know what they said to Mary, but whatever it was, she remembered it forever. Words here and there can keep us going: a word of love, a word of advice, a word of prayer. Remember a time when a person you loved spoke your name—this is the word of the Lord!

O Wisdom,
Lord and Ruler,
Root of Jesse,
Key of David,
Rising Sun,
King of the Nations,
Emmanuel, Come Jesus.

Conclusion
Look back over the retreat
During this Advent retreat, we have encountered the unique and surpassing joy of God, embodied in the birth of Christ. Through the words of Isaiah and the eyes of Zechariah, Elizabeth, Mary, Joseph, and the shepherds, we have experienced the anticipation, the Advent, that preceded this magnificent act of love. We can now take time to reflect on this retreat, and, as Mary treasured the events and pondered them in her

heart, we too can recall what we have learned and begin to discover how we might become messengers of joy.

Before you conclude this retreat, you might ask Jesus to help you hold on to the graces you have received. Was your heart moved when you prayed? Was there a Scripture reading or image that particularly resonated with you? Perhaps you received a new insight into the meaning of God's gift of joy. If you were to pray with the text of the retreat again, what line or phrase would you go back to?

In the second week of his Spiritual Exercises, Ignatius of Loyola says that contemplating the mystery of Christmas means "seeing in imagination the way from Nazareth to Bethlehem." Ignatius suggests that you picture the Nativity scene in your mind and "consider, observe, and contemplate what the persons are saying." After this, he proposes, you might reflect on this mystery "and draw some fruit from it." Spend a few moments now pondering the Bethlehem scene. Jesus is born in a humble stable, to a poor family among the ordinary people of the time. Simple shepherds were the first witnesses to this event. Enter the silence of this scene. Ask yourself, What does it mean for me?

Jesus, God-made-man, who was born in such simple surroundings, desires to come into the most ordinary events of our daily life. This is the true message of Christmas: Emmanuel—God with us—comes to us in the depths of our hearts and invites us to meet him there. We are his beloved sons and daughters, and we can encounter him everywhere: in our homes and our workplaces, in silence or in speech, on our own or with our friends, in the beauty of the countryside or the bustle of city life. Where are you most conscious of Jesus' presence? Let him gaze at you now and speak to him from your heart about how the experience of this retreat has been for you. Share with him your joys and sorrows, your hopes and fears.

Looking to the times that lie ahead, think about how this retreat may help you. What has stayed with you? What might be useful to hold on to? Have you experienced a particular blessing or sense of joy during this time? Where have you met challenges or difficulties? Have you felt resistance? What are you most looking forward to? As Christmas and the new year approach, ask Jesus for the grace of being fully alive to his presence. Ask him for the help, strength, and joy you need for the future. Conscious that you are on this journey together, come closer to Jesus now and offer these final moments of prayer to him.

Suscipe

Take, Lord, and receive all my liberty,
my memory, my understanding,
and my entire will,

all I have and call my own.
You have given all to me.

To you, Lord, I return it.
Everything is yours; do with it what you will.
Give me only your love and your grace;
that is enough for me.

—St. Ignatius of Loyola

Prayer to Know God's Will

May it please the supreme and divine Goodness
To give us all abundant grace
Ever to know his most holy will
And perfectly to fulfill it.

—St. Ignatius of Loyola